A KICK-ASS GUIDE TO
Smarter Money Habits

Fresh ideas to transform your money habits TODAY and put your money to work for YOU; live on less, pay off debt, retire with more!

K.M. MacVey

Copyright © 2019 K.M. MacVey

All rights reserved.

ISBN-13: 9781678511098

Table of Contents

Introduction III

CHAPTER 1 – HABITS FOR BUDGETING 1

Why you need a budget 2
Set up a budget 2
Use a budgeting tool 3

CHAPTER 2 – HABITS FOR GOAL-SETTING 8

Set short-term goals 8
Set long-term goals 12

CHAPTER 3 – HABITS THAT BUST YOUR BUDGET 15

Manage spending triggers 15

CHAPTER 4 – HABITS THAT CUT COSTS 19

Housing 19
Utilities 21
Transportation 23
Insurance 24
Groceries 25
Financial Services 28
Medical 29
Clothing and Shoes 31
Miscellaneous 31

CHAPTER 5 – HABITS FOR BOOSTING INCOME 35

On the job 35
Passive income options 36
Sell your old stuff 38

CHAPTER 6 – HABITS TO REDUCE DEBT 39

Consolidation loans 39
0% credit card transfers 40
Paydown methods 40

CHAPTER 7 – HABITS FOR SAVING AND INVESTING 42

Establish an emergency fund 42
Invest for retirement 43
Automate savings and investments 44
Don't give away free money 44

WRAP-UP 46

RESOURCES 47

Introduction

Congratulations for taking steps to learn some new money habits that can help you reach your goals!! I've written this book to pass along some of what I've learned about personal money management. Only 5 years ago, my family was facing more than $100,000 of medical and consumer debt. No money saved. No investments. In my mid-50s, we had only my rather small pension from 27 years of teaching and a good job. My spouse was unable to work following a traumatic brain injury, so I was desperate to take charge and improve our financial situation, knowing that if we didn't make big changes I would be working until the day I died.

To rescue the idea of retiring one day, I took on every cost-cutting method I could think of – and researched further to find even more ways to stretch the paycheck. We cut costs dramatically by moving to an inexpensive, rural area. We worked hard to pay off debt and save - investing for the first time in either of our lives. Today – 5 years later - we have not only climbed out of that debt we now have a net worth well over $100,000. There is hope for retirement!

I know there are many of you out there living paycheck-to-paycheck barely making ends meet and some of you may be approaching retirement desperate for some fresh ideas on reducing costs so you can save more and feel comfortable making the decision to retire. Regardless of your income, there are things you can do to improve your financial situation. This book is for you.

In the first few chapters of the book, I'll share information about some good budgeting and goal-setting habits. You'll learn about tools to set up a budget that matches your circumstances and meets your goals. I've also included tips on how to avoid some common spending traps to help you stick to your budget.

Next, I'll discuss habits to cut spending in every category of your budget and take steps to increase your income. Some of these cost-cutting measures may be common sense, and some may be things that have never occurred to you! What is most important to you and your family may be different than someone else so it is completely up to you to make the decisions about where to cut spending in your budget from amongst all the ideas presented so you can afford what *you* really care about.

The last part of the book will discuss some tips on how to use some of that money you've trimmed from your budget to efficiently pay down debt so you are able to save and invest. Live links to resources are embedded throughout the text and compiled on the resources page found at the end of the book. Check out the ones that interest you. Keep in mind that some of the ideas in this book would work well for some people and maybe not for others. You have many choices. Take what works for you and leave the rest. After all, it is YOUR money!

Chapter 1 – Habits for Budgeting

Probably the most important money habit that will allow you to keep more of the money you make is budgeting. Boring and tedious at times, but necessary. Some of you might be making a budget for the very first time. If that's the case, good for you! I didn't make a budget at all until I was in my 30's. However, I did track my spending as it seems I was always broke. Probably because I didn't have a budget!

If you're like me, your parents never taught you anything about money management and there were no opportunities to learn about it in school. I have spent most of my career working 2-3 jobs to make ends meet because I had bad money habits that I wasn't even aware of. For years, I searched out some workable solutions to my financial dilemma because life is too short to spend it all working! So, I've spent a lot of time researching and learning about what can be done to improve my own personal finance situation. I want to share some of what I've learned with you.

Why you need a budget

You NEED a budget!! Regardless of your income. Some propose that you stick to an "ideal budget" with specific percentages of your income set aside for housing, utilities, and the like. But this does not take into consideration the fact that people's needs change depending on their income level, whether they live in urban or rural communities, whether they have children or pets, and what stage of life they are in. Also, I don't think most of us think about our income and spending in terms of percent, we think about it in terms of dollars and cents. So, I disagree with the ideal budget philosophy as a "one-size-fits-all" approach. Instead, I propose that you let your priorities dictate what proportion of your budget should go towards each budget category.

You might be thinking, why do you even need a budget? Well, so you can decide – ahead of time – what you will do with your paycheck before it even hits the bank. If you don't decide, who will? When you make a dedicated plan to take care of priority needs first, you can make long and short-term savings goals for things you really want. Like a bigger house. New car. European vacation. Retirement. You get the idea. Some of you may have a budget – sort of – in your head, and still others may have a well-organized workable budget. If you have a system that works for you already, feel free to skip this part of the book!

Set up a budget

Here are a few simple steps on how to get started with a first budget if you've never budgeted before:
1. First, look at all your expenses and income month-to-month on the past year's monthly bank statements. If you don't keep cash, this is an accurate reflection of total income and spending.

2. Then, calculate a monthly average for each type of expense (housing, utilities, transportation, insurance, groceries, medical, clothing, etc.) and document these averages. You could use an Excel spreadsheet for this OR you could easily do it on paper just to get started.
3. For more occasional costs such as car repair, license renewals and the like – divide the total annual costs by 12 to get a monthly average. Evaluate your spending and notice where your money is going.
4. Ask yourself if your money is going where you think it is or where you want it to. Decide if you need to make any adjustments according to your spending priorities.
5. Each month revisit your actual spending and adjust your budget categories, as needed, for the next month.

You can use any number of top-rated apps to help you track your spending. I've included an overview of some of these in the next section. I use the Excel spreadsheet for our budget. I like that I can keep budgets from multiple years and see how spending habits evolve. I also use the Mint app as it gives me a bigger picture of our total financial situation at a glance. At any time, I can see an updated picture of net worth, property values, investments, total debts, total cash from all my accounts at once. This ability has helped us more accurately set goals and track progress towards those goals on a monthly basis.

There are other budgeting tools that are widely used that you may be interested in learning about. Check out some information about Excel and Mint and some of the other top-rated budgeting apps in the following section.

Use a budgeting tool

There are many personal finance tools available. I've investigated some of the more popular choices. You can set up a budget using any of these software tools:
- Microsoft Excel
- Mint (free)
- YNAB
- Mvelopes

- Quicken
- Moneydance
- CountAbout
- Personal Capital (free)

Here's just a little bit of information about each of these so you can decide which of them you'd like to explore further.

Microsoft Excel

Most of you are probably familiar with Microsoft Excel - a spreadsheet program developed by Microsoft for Windows, macOS, Android and iOS. Some of the more useful features include the ability to perform a wide variety of calculations and produce multiple types of graphs. You can pay for Excel as part of the Microsoft Office package that also includes Word, PowerPoint, Outlook, Publisher and Access.

The Microsoft Office Personal version (1-person access) is currently $69.99 per year or you can choose to pay 6.99 monthly. Or, if you prefer, you can pay a bit more for the Home version (access for 6) at $99.99 per year or $9.99 monthly. Current offers include a free trial month with this option.

If you don't want the entire Microsoft Office package, you can purchase Excel as a stand-alone for somewhat less. The software license does allow you to install on up to 5 devices and includes an app for your phone.

The benefits of using Excel are many. It's been around since 2000 and was part of the initial software package on most computers for many years. So, there are lots of resources out there such as video tutorials, courses, etc. for help. Another benefit is the ability to add additional sheets to the workbook. This allows you to track your budgets for as many years as you like. Also, many people such as myself have used the program for other purposes and feel comfortable with it, so why not use it for personal budgeting as well?

Mint

Mint is a free budgeting app developed by Intuit, the people behind TurboTax. Mint allows you to connect all your accounts in one place and choose the dollar amounts to put into each category of the budget. Then, as you spend, the app shows how much remains of each category budget in both a visual and numerical display. I really love that it does this! At any moment in time you can look and see how much money is remaining in any of your budget categories.

Other benefits include your credit score information displayed and updated monthly for free and ongoing calculation of your net worth. Mint also refreshes all your linked account information every time you log in. The app is flexible in that the categories set up in the budget can easily be changed to meet your individual needs. A downside to the Mint app is because it is free, you put up with a lot of annoying ads. If you want to try it out, you can go to Mint.com and set up a free account on your computer, then download the free Mint app from the app store on your phone.

You Need a Budget (YNAB)

Better known by its acronym YNAB, You Need a Budget is another solid possibility. This personal finance app will run on both Windows and Mac and allows data sharing between users. Like Mint, it's a browser-based program that will also sync to an app on your phone.

Designed for beginners, this program has some cool benefits. For instance, it intuitively guides you to follow good budgeting practices and even has a feature that will alert you if you stray too far off the budget you've set. For those of you who tried to budget in the past and failed, this could be the perfect app for you. It will cost you a little, however. Current price is $7.00 a month. Check it out for yourself at youneedabudget.com.

Mvelopes

If you've always hoped for a digital version of the old envelope budgeting system, Mvelopes may be just the app you want. How it works is you decide how much cash to put in envelopes for each budget category, label the envelope with what the cash is for, and when you've spent it all, your envelope will light up red. Like Mint and YNAB, Mvelopes is a web-based program that also includes mobile apps so you can sync to all your accounts.

Three different versions are available for you to choose from: Mvelopes Basic, Mvelopes Plus, and Mvelopes Complete. Mvelopes Basic is priced at $6/month and comes with a free trial, the Plus is $19/month and gives you access to a virtual learning center, debt center, and a quarterly check in with a coach. The Plus package is $59/month. Plus is a guided program, including a monthly consultation with a personal finance coach. You can find Mvelopes online at www.mvelopes.com.

Quicken

Most of you are familiar with the Quicken name – it's been around for decades in software packages for personal or business finance. So, you may find it seems a bit old-fashioned in some ways. Quicken does everything you'd expect a personal budgeting app to do - and does them well. Like the other apps we've discussed, Quicken syncs the information from all your financial accounts in one place, and tracks your spending categories for you. Quicken is available in multiple versions, so you'll have to check out which would best fit your needs. Currently, there are three different plans for Mac users that run $35–$68 per year and four different plans for Windows that are priced between $35–$90 per year. Check out these choices at www.quicken.com.

Moneydance

Moneydance may be a name that's new to you. This app is essentially a Quicken app on steroids for Mac users, compatible with Windows, macOS, and Linux. It does everything that you'd expect from a personal finance app, helping you to set up a budget and make charts and graphs to help track your spending.

It also does a few very useful things that most other personal finance budgeting apps don't. Moneydance has built-in online banking – allowing you to pay bills and manage your accounts right there in the app. Moneydance also tracks your investment performance and is a great tool for those who have foreign accounts as it can handle multiple currencies, including cryptocurrency.

Beginners may find Moneydance overwhelming with everything it has to offer, so it may be a better choice for more experienced personal money managers. Moneydance offers a free app for your iPhone or Android that will sync with your desktop instantly. The current price is $49.99 but they do offer a free trial with a 90- day money-back guarantee if you aren't satisfied for any reason. You'll find Moneydance online at moneydance.com.

CountAbout

CountAbout is the only web-based app that can import data directly from either Quicken or Mint so you don't lose your information when you switch apps. You can also use this app on the go. Mobile apps are available for both iOS and Android which sync your information automatically.

Two plans are offered: Basic, at $9.99 a year, and Premium, at $39.99 a year. The Basic plan does not automatically download transactions from your financial institutions and does not support Quicken's Direct Connect. However, you can upload them manually. If you want an app that automatically connects to your financial institutions and downloads your transactions, choose Premium. A free 15-day trial is offered to the Premium plan. For more features, you can pay extra to have images uploaded or add an invoicing feature. Go to countabout.com for more information.

Personal Capital

Personal Capital is a budgeting tool that lets you import transactions from your various accounts, just like most others. The app has a list of budgeting categories that unfortunately you cannot edit. Like many of the other apps, you can create charts and graphs for both spending and savings data, comparing your budget numbers from one week or one month to the next.

Like Mint, Personal Capital also calculates your net worth and includes some free investing tools so you can monitor the market and track your all your investments in one place. An extra perk this app offers is tracking broker fees and alerting you to hidden fees. All in all, Personal Capital is a solid budgeting app that offers more tools to someone focused on building wealth through investments. The Personal Capital app is free, although they do offer a premium version for more personal attention from a registered financial advisor

Chapter 2 – Habits for Goal-setting

You've set up a budget and are tracking your spending. What's next? Short answer - setting some goals for yourself. Short-term AND long-term goals.

Consider your current state of affairs and ask yourself these questions. Is your money going towards wants or needs? Is your spending in line with your priorities? Do you have debt? How much? Do you have an emergency fund? Are you contributing to savings and investments? Do you have enough insurance?

Set short-term goals

Generally, short-term goals are anything that can be accomplished in a year or less. Let's look at some potential short-term goals you might consider:
- Creating a budget
- Automating your finances
- Improving your credit score
- Trimming your spending in one or more areas
- Getting quotes on insurance to find a lower price or better coverage
- Paying off a debt
- Transferring credit card balances to a 0% card

- Setting up a new savings account at a higher rate
- Refinancing a large debt (e.g. Auto or Mortgage) for a shorter term or lower rate
- Saving for a vacation or larger purchase
- Setting up or contributing to an emergency fund
- Starting or contributing to a Health Savings Account or Flexible Savings Account
- Starting or contributing to a college savings plan
- Starting or contributing to a retirement plan
- Asking for a raise or applying for a promotion at work
- Taking on a part-time gig for extra cash

Now don't try to do all of these at the same time! For most of us, it's more effective to choose no more than 3-5 goals to focus on. Think about choosing 1-2 goals that can increase how much money you have left over at the end of the month (trim spending, pay off a debt, refinance a debt, ask for a raise, etc.) and then 1-2 goals for using that money to more effectively meet your needs according to your priorities (emergency fund, HSA/FSA, saving for retirement).

Keep a record of your annual goals in writing so you are always reminded of what you have decided to work towards. I record short-term goals on the Excel budget sheet so I see it every month when I enter information on the budget.

Set up a budget

In Chapter 1, I gave you some tips on setting up a budget. If you haven't done it yet, get on it!

Automate

Once you have a solid budget set up, you may immediately see some areas that you can automate and some you can trim. In very little time, you can set up automatic mortgage and bill payments, savings deposits, and investment contributions with online bill pay directly from your checking account. Automation helps save you time and stick to your goals! If you don't ever see the money, you are less likely to miss it.

Improve your credit score

The interest rates you pay on loans, credit cards, and insurance products depend on your credit score. Take steps to improve it. Pay down or pay off a debt, make sure you pay all your bills on time, use less than 30% of your available credit, and apply for credit sparingly to improve your score. Check your score at least annually and look for any errors in the reports from the 3 credit bureaus TransUnion, Equifax, and Experian. If you do find errors, these could be lowering your score and you should dispute them.

Trim spending
Notice some areas of the budget you are spending more than you want? In Chapter 4 you'll find many cost-cutting ideas for all the different areas of your budget.

Invest in Insurance
Insurance is expensive, but necessary. Consider the cost of car repairs if you got in a wreck and had no insurance. Could you pay for a significant repair bill? For most of us, the answer is probably not. Insurance is designed to save you from the catastrophic costs that you would have to pay if you didn't have it.

What about life insurance? Do you have loved ones who depend on your income for a roof over their head and food on the table? Make sure you have enough life insurance to provide for them 3-5 years of salary, pay burial costs, and cover your debts should anything happen to you. The good news is that pricing structures at different insurance companies change periodically so it's important to get multiple quotes from different companies at least once a year to see if you can get a better rate, better coverage, or both. You may decide that you need to increase your coverage. This would be a great time for a new quote!

Pay off a debt
Do you have a debt you could pay off in a year or less? Take the balance you owe, divide it by 12 and then make monthly installments to get rid of that debt!

Transfer credit card balances to 0% card
You may periodically receive notices from one or more of your credit card accounts of an opportunity to transfer balances at 0%. Most of the time, these offers come with a significant transfer fee of 4%, 5% or even more. However, if you are currently paying an interest rate higher than that and are given at least a year at the 0% rate, GO FOR IT! This may save you enough in interest charges over the year that you can significantly pay the balance down on that account, if not pay it off. This payoff strategy is described more fully in Chapter 5.

Open a high-rate savings account

Are you getting less than 0.1% interest on your savings account? You can do better! Go to Bankrate.com to see current interest rates and terms on the best savings accounts. Many online banks offer better than 2% rates. That's 20 times the interest you're currently earning! Be careful to examine the terms of the account carefully and minimum balances required before you apply.

Refinance a large debt

If you have significant equity in a home or auto, you can refinance! And if your credit rating is better than it was before and/or the interest rates are lower, you can save an impressive amount of money every month – for years!

Save for a vacation or large purchase

Put your savings on autopilot as mentioned above. Set an amount every month to automatically move from your paycheck directly into your savings account. If you don't see it, you won't miss it!

Try a savings app

Need an app to help you save a little more? Try Acorns. Acorns is an app designed to save and invest your spare change for you - automatically. The Acorns app tracks your purchases from debit and credit card transactions and rounds them up to the nearest dollar. The difference in change is then invested for you in safe ETF portfolios. For example, if you spend $6.80 at the gas station, the purchase is rounded up to $7.00 and the $.20 is invested in your portfolio of choice. Each transaction is such a small amount that it's unlikely you will ever miss the money.

Unfortunately, unless you are a college student it is not free to use the app, though I doubt anyone will flinch at the cost. The basic plan costs $1 per month with a portfolio value less than $5,000. Over $5000? Then it costs 0.25% of your balance. This basic plan is centered around moving your spare change into investments. There are two other available plans as well. The second plan is $2 per month and helps you with investing and saving for retirement. The third plan is $3 per month and includes investing, saving for retirement, and Acorns new debit card and checking account known as Acorns Spend.

Establish an emergency Fund

The standard advice is to have at least 3-6 months' income saved in an emergency fund. This saves you from using credit when those annoying extra expenses crop up (it's always something, isn't it?).

Open a Health Savings Account or Flexible Savings Account
These two types of savings accounts allow you to put away money monthly for health-related expenses tax-free. Over time, this savings strategy alone can save you a significant sum of money, as the cost of healthcare continues to rise.

Contribute to a college savings plan
Are there children in your family that you're saving money for college expenses? Consider setting up contributions to a tax-advantaged, low-fee 529 plan. Earnings used for qualified expenses are TAX-FREE!

Contribute to a retirement plan
Do you ever want to retire? Unless you do plan on working until you die, you will need cash for retirement. The earlier you start saving for it, the better – thanks to compound interest. Even a small sum contributed monthly can grow into a large nest egg given enough time. Use that to your advantage!

Ask for a raise or promotion
The fastest way to increase your monthly paycheck is to get a raise or promotion. Many people are too afraid to ask, even though they are deserving of a raise. What will it hurt to ask?

Take on a part-time gig
There are many part-time opportunities, even remote jobs you can do at home you can take on for some extra monthly cash. If you have a specific savings goal but can't meet it with your current pay, consider taking on a part-time gig. Even a few hours a month may make enough of a difference!

Set long-term goals

Long-term goals are those things we want to accomplish over several years' time. Meeting your short-term goals should support the pursuit of your long-term goals. Here are a few possibilities you might consider:

- Debt elimination

- Paying for college
- Retirement fund
- Travel
- Dream house
- Giving

Eliminate debt

Debt is perhaps the biggest thing standing in the way of you ever having any wealth to speak of. Probably the first long-term goal you need to set is a plan for paying it all off – including a mortgage, if you have one.

Save for college

For parents of college-bound children, having enough money socked away to pay for their college is an uphill climb as college tuition and fees continue to soar. A worthy long-term goal is having the funds saved by the time they are needed.

Maximize your retirement fund

This may be the longest-term goal of the bunch and one that's difficult to plan for. You won't really know how long you want to continue to work until you get there, and there are many variables to consider. Will you have a pension? IRA? 401K from work? Social security? Regardless, you will at minimum need to consider having enough money saved on your own to take care of medical costs in retirement (some current estimates at $300,000 and up!) and potentially long-term care.

Travel

Do you have dreams of traveling? Many people do! If you want to travel before or after retirement, you will need the funds saved to do so. Consider this when you're thinking about long-term goals.

Dream house

What about that dream house you've always wanted? Will you be able to afford it when the time comes? Have the down-payment saved up so you can live in that dream house!

Giving

A long-term goal for many is philanthropy. Giving from the labor of your life to enrich the community around you is a very worthy goal. Most of you reading this probably also want something to pass along to children or grandchildren when you're gone. Things for you to consider as you make long-term financial goals.

Chapter 3 –Habits That Bust Your Budget

Manage spending triggers

A spending trigger is a place or situation in which you find yourself regularly overspending. Strong emotions such as feeling happy, sad, anxious, or bored can influence your spending patterns and lead many to overspend. If this becomes a regular habit, overspending – even in small ways – can destroy your budget and prevent you from reaching your goals. It is possible to identify your spending triggers and find ways to avoid or reduce the damage to the budget.

Are there places you go that you know you will spend too much? For me, it's the bookstore. I can't just go and look. I will buy something – Every. Time. It's also eating out. I love to go out to eat. I also tend to overspend on our pets. And I have another trigger - if I carry cash, I will spend it. ALL! And usually all in one place. Finally, I know not to go into a grocery store if I am hungry or I will buy everything in sight!

So, think about your daily routines and where you spend money perhaps a little too loosely. You can recognize the triggers by keeping close tabs on your monthly budget. Are there ways of avoiding your triggers or at least limiting yourself if you know you have a trigger?

Since I know what my triggers are, I have developed ways of dealing with them. To avoid overspending at the bookstore, I have gotten myself a public library card and I have a Kindle. I can read pretty much anything now for free or next to nothing. Going to the library is just as enjoyable to me as browsing through a bookstore - only the books are FREE! This has solved my bookstore addiction.

When we go out to eat, I limit my spending to a certain dollar amount that's in line with the budget. Sometimes this means going somewhere less expensive but I'm OK with that. What I really enjoy about eating out is the experience and the company. It doesn't have to be expensive to be a pleasant experience.

Finally, I never carry cash. Never. Ever. Because I know I will spend it. It "burns a hole in my pocket" as some might say. So, I just don't. You do need to have some pleasures in life – but they don't always have to cost a lot of money and they need to be planned for, so you have money for the more important things in your budget.

Here's a list of just a few typical spending triggers that cause many people to overspend:

- You've had a tough day and feel you deserve some "retail therapy"
- You're feeling lazy and don't want to fix your own meal
- You overspend when you're with friends
- Holidays and birthdays
- Grandchildren
- Pets
- Breakup with a loved one
- A new relationship
- Online shopping
- Bars and restaurants
- Loss of a job
- Grocery shopping while hungry

Do you see any of these situations that trigger overspending for you? Recognizing that you have a spending trigger is the first step! See if you can think of ways to minimize the damage by changing behavior patterns. Avoid situations that cause you to overspend whenever possible. If the situation cannot be avoided, plan to limit your spending to keep it in line with your budget as best you can.

Many of our over-indulgences can be avoided and our budget rescued if we are a little more careful about planning. When you don't plan, you could pay dearly for it! Conveniences that save us time usually cost us more money.

Plan ahead

Are you one of those people who goes inside for a snack and a drink when you stop for gas? Those same items bought from a convenience store or gas station probably cost twice what you would have paid for them at a grocery store. Go to the grocery store and have snacks and drinks on hand so when you are traveling you can take them with you.

Do you shop with a list or do you just wander up and down the aisles in the grocery store, picking out what you want? Resist the urge to impulse buy items you don't really need by making a list before you go to the grocery store and then stick to buying only what is on the list.

A classic example of a money drain is splurging on expensive coffee because you didn't take 5 minutes to make it yourself. I've got to admit – I am a coffee snob and like a quality cup of joe. But I don't hit my local coffee shop every morning. Instead I buy quality roasted coffee beans, grind them myself and make my own coffee. You can buy fresh roasted coffee beans at most local grocers and grind them right there at the store if you like. It is delicious, I get to enjoy a great cup of coffee and don't pay but a small fraction of the price I would pay at the coffee shop.

What do you do for lunch? Do you take a lunch with you to work made from home or do you "wing it" and go out for lunch because you didn't take the time to make yourself lunch? Going out to lunch will cost you 3-10 times as much as it would cost you to make your own and bring it from home. Changing this one habit alone can save you hundreds of dollars a year!

Do you cook meals at home, or do you rely on take-out or going out to restaurants? If time is a factor, do your meal preparations on the weekend and freeze meal-size portions for the week. Decide ahead of time what meals you want to prepare and shop for the ingredients, so you have them on hand. You can make the process fun by involving the whole family and trying some different recipes.

Plan for specials and discounts

Look out for specials and discounts on services like auto maintenance and repair, haircuts and dry cleaning. You can save 25% or more if you take advantage of these discounts.

Insurance plans typically offer a discounted rate if you pay quarterly, semi-annually, or annually instead of choosing to pay monthly. You can typically save 10% or more.

Do you go to sporting events, movies, theater and music shows, museums or amusement parks? Look online for discounts to these and many other types of entertainment venues. Often, a venue will have a regular showtime or day of the week that they offer discounted rates. A few minutes of your time investigating these possibilities can save you a bundle – especially if you're paying for a family.

If you're interested in purchasing a membership to a gym or club, see if they offer discounted fees or rates before you commit. Many fitness chains offer discounted fees at certain times of the year and reduced rates for a couple or family membership.

Chapter 4 – Habits that Cut Costs

OK, here's the part of the book many of you have been waiting for - ideas to slash costs in every area of your budget. Not all these ideas save big dollar amounts by themselves, but keep in mind that everything you do to save - even the little things - will ADD UP. Enjoy :)

Housing

Housing is by far your biggest bill every month, regardless if you rent or buy. If you already have a mortgage, there are ways to reduce what you pay. When interest rates are low, consider refinancing. You can often reduce the monthly payment and the length of the loan, saving you money both now AND later.

Shop for a lender. Get at least 3 quotes before you commit. Don't be afraid to haggle – if you can get a better deal with one lender, see if another will match or beat it. Even a small percentage difference makes a huge difference in total dollars spent over the life of a mortgage.

Make sure your FICO credit score is very good, 740 or better before you apply for credit. The interest rate you get on a mortgage can cause your payment to differ by hundreds of dollars a month depending on your credit score. It's a good idea to check your 3 credit scores a few months before you apply for a new mortgage or a refinance, so you know what your score is and have some time to improve it or dispute errors you find. It costs nothing to get your credit score from all 3 credit bureaus (TransUnion, Equifax, Experian) once a year and checking it has no impact on your score. Order your scores free at annualcreditreport.com.

Save up as large a down payment as you can. The more cash you can pay up front means the less debt you will have to accrue interest over 15 or 30 years. You can save thousands over the long run by making a larger down payment. By putting at least 20% down, you can avoid the added cost of Private Mortgage Insurance (PMI).

Choose a shorter loan term if you can. Generally, you can get a much better interest rate on a 15-year loan than a comparable 30-year loan and save yourself thousands of dollars in the long run.

Once your mortgage loan balance drops below 80% of the home value, you can drop Private Mortgage Insurance (PMI) from your payments, if you are currently paying it. Depending on the value of your home, that can be a huge amount! Typical PMI rates are as much as $125/month on a $200,000 mortgage. That's $1500 a year you can save!

When refinancing is not an option and you are more concerned with reducing the length of your mortgage and the total amount you will pay, this is easily done by paying a little bit more towards your principal every month. You can pay off a 30-year mortgage earlier by taking advantage of this tip. One extra full payment a year can cut a 30-year mortgage down to about 15 years.

Apply for your county's homestead exemption program. By claiming your property as your primary residence, you can save hundreds to thousands a year on your property taxes. If you are over 65, most counties offer additional programs to freeze your property taxes. Be sure to investigate and apply for these as soon as you're eligible.

If you are considering moving to reduce your housing bill, look at properties further out from a city center. Rural properties tend to be less expensive per square foot and often have septic systems and wells on the property that can also save on utilities. Or you could downsize to a smaller home, condo, or apartment. Tiny homes and RVs are more popular than ever as people try to make their housing dollar stretch further.

Especially attractive if you work remotely, you might consider moving to one of the places that will pay you to move and/or live there. Believe it or not – there are places that offer these incentives! Currently, you can get a free plot of land for a home or business or other significant perks to pick up and move to any one of these places:
- Flagler, Colorado
- Marne, Iowa
- Tribune, Kansas
- Curtis, Nebraska
- Harmony, Minnesota
- Cheyenne, Wyoming
- Baltimore, Maryland

Utilities

If you live in an urban area, you likely are receiving water, trash, electrical, cable/wireless, and phone services. For some of these services, you may not have any choice of providers depending on the municipality in which you live. For those services which you have a choice of providers, shop around to both compare prices and look at reviews. Often, a provider will offer a special introductory rate to new customers for a specified period that can bring down your total cost for the year.

TV services
If you can do without a TV service at all, you can save yourself a hefty monthly bill. We recently stopped our cable TV and bought an HD antenna for about $30, swapping a monthly $75 bill for no monthly bill. We get about 50 channels with the antenna and do not miss the cable TV. Others enjoy streaming services like Netflix, Hulu, Sling and others. Bundling several of these services can easily bring your total bill up beyond what it was with cable, so do your due diligence when considering these.

Phone

Examine your cell phone usage. Are you paying for more data than you use? Do you really need an unlimited data plan? Check out your current provider's and the competition's plans and prices. You may be able to get by with a cheaper plan. We recently switched cell phone providers because we found a competitor that only charges for data by the gig – all calls and texts are free. Our cell phone bill plummeted from over $175 a month to just over $28 a month. If you are still paying for a landline but never use it, consider dropping it altogether.

Water
The water bill may be one of those utilities that you don't have the option to choose among providers. You can still cut costs by up to 1/3 by reducing your usage. Luckily, there are LOTS of ways to cut water usage. Here are a few:
- Check for faucet, toilet or pipe leaks and repair any you find
- Install low flow toilets and showerheads
- Run only full loads of laundry
- Run the dishwasher only when full
- Avoid hand-washing dishes
- Use high efficiency appliances (He) to save both water and energy
- Install low flow aerators in your faucets
- Don't leave water running when brushing your teeth
- Take shorter showers
- Insulate water pipes to reduce time to get heated water to the faucet
- Don't water the lawn more than once a week
- Xeriscape your yard

Electricity
Depending on where you live, you may be able to choose an electricity provider. If you can choose among providers, compare the plans and rates offered by each one and check out the reviews left by customers before you decide. Sometimes, electric companies also offer introductory deals to new customers which may be worth your time to investigate. These aren't always a good deal in the long term, so be sure to check their rates before you switch.

You can also cut electricity costs by reducing your usage. Here are many ideas to help you do that:
- Insulation
- Use weather stripping and caulk around windows and doors
- Replace windows with double-pane Energy Star windows

- Use carpet and rugs to insulate floors and keep heat in
- Add insulation in your attic
- Appliances
- Use high efficiency appliances
- Microwave or grill instead of using the stove or oven
- Run washer and dishwasher only when full
- Don't use the heat-dry cycle on dishwasher
- Wash laundry on cold cycle as often as possible
- Clean lint tray on dryer after every load
- Turn down the temperature on your water heater
- HVAC
- Use a programmable thermostat
- Get an annual tune up on your HVAC system
- Replace air filters monthly
- Turn heat down in winter 4 degrees, AC up in summer 4 degrees
- Use ceiling fans – clockwise in winter, counter-clockwise in summer
- Close blinds and shades in summer to reduce heat build-up
- Lighting
- Switch out old light bulbs with energy-saving LEDs
- Turn off lights and appliances when not in use
- Use solar-powered lights outdoors

Transportation

Do you own multiple vehicles? Can you get by without one of them? Transportation costs are a considerable chunk out of your budget every month. When you consider all of the costs involved with owning a vehicle – loan or lease payment, insurance, registration fees, gas, upkeep and maintenance – it can save you a bundle if you can use mass transit or ride-share to avoid keeping an extra vehicle.

If you cannot rid yourself of a vehicle, you can reduce your total transportation costs by establishing some of these habits:

- Refinancing a vehicle loan
- Trading in an expensive vehicle for a smaller, economical one
- Buy a good used car instead of new
- Shop around for financing options
- Avoiding toll roads
- Keeping credit scores high to lower insurance costs
- Getting annual insurance quotes
- Doing preventive maintenance to avoid or reduce major repair bills
- Shopping around for lower gas prices
- Using discounted services and coupons for oil changes and repairs
- Driving safely to avoid accidents and tickets

Along with the many steps you can take to lower your everyday transportation costs, there are also ways to save on flying, rental cars, and hotels. Booking travel through a discount site such as Travelocity, Expedia, Priceline, Orbitz, TripAdvisor and others can save you big bucks – some advertised deals give you a 40%, 50%, or even 60% discount. Be aware that some airlines may not honor their refund/change policy if the reservation is booked through a travel website.

Insurance

There are several ways you can save on insurance. If you have more than one policy, bundling them together can save you – a LOT. Also keep in mind that insurance rates are affected by your credit score. A higher credit score can get you a lower rate. Factors such as paying your bills on time, maintaining a mix of credit types (mortgage, short-term loans, credit cards) and limiting the number of credit applications in a year can help you keep a higher credit score.

Consider paying for insurance on a quarterly, semi-annual, or annual basis if your company offers those choices. Depending on the company, doing this alone can save you 10% or more.

The last tip I have for you to lower your insurance bill is to get new quotes at least once every year. Rates do change periodically, and this is a simple way of making sure you are getting the best deal possible. You can get free quotes for multiple companies at www.nerdwallet.com/insurance.

Groceries

Your food/grocery bill is one of the places you can cut costs dramatically. Our crazy, busy lives give us good reason to search out the products which are most convenient and save us time. We run through the store, grabbing what we want and don't always consider the costs of what we end up with in our shopping cart.

Many people struggle with keeping to a grocery budget, but it can be done if you know some cost-saving tips. We cut our food bill nearly in half by following the tips described in this section.

Make a list and stick to it

Remember those spending triggers we talked about? Many of us have food spending triggers, well, because who doesn't like food? Make a list of those items needed for the week and don't buy anything not on your list. Beware of going grocery shopping when you're hungry – those spending triggers will kick in! Need help making a list? Try the Anylist app. Just say or type in the item you want to add to the list. You can share your list with anyone so family or friends can see and add to your list!

Don't waste food

It is estimated that over 30% of the food that is purchased in this country goes to waste. Have storage containers and bags available to store leftovers and only buy perishable goods in quantities you will use short-term. A great investment is a Food Saver vacuum sealer. This handy gadget helps reduce your overall food costs by keeping your food fresh up to 5 times longer. You can vacuum seal just about any food to keep in refrigerator or freezer.

Avoid buying prepared meals

Whether canned, boxed, or frozen, prepared meals can save time but can cost upwards of 3-10 times what we would pay to prepare the same meal from scratch. Often, the prepared meals don't even save you that much time. Another benefit of preparing meals at home is that you can make enough to have leftovers to freeze for another time. Take advantage of this and do your cooking when you have the time (maybe the weekend?) and freeze meal-size portions.

Comparison shop

If there are more than one choice of grocery store in your area, compare the prices between them. If you have the time to visit more than one store to get the best prices on everything you need, do it! Not everyone has this luxury, however.

Compare per-item prices

You can still save, even if you do all your shopping at one store. Compare the per-item prices on different size packages and between brands. Sometimes this will surprise you. You might think that a larger package of something might always be the better buy, but that's not always the case. Recently I bought some walnuts that were packaged in 3 different sized packages. The smallest package cost half the amount per ounce as either of the other 2 sizes. I confess – it surprised me that there was such a big difference in price just due to the size of the package!

Pay attention to expiration dates

Ever gotten home and realized you had purchased something that was already expired? Frustrating, isn't it? Take the time to notice expiration dates on perishable items. Avoid making any purchases of items you won't be able to use or freeze before they expire.

Buy produce in-season

Fruits and vegetables are often available year-round but will be most expensive when they are out of season. Choose the in-season varieties for lower prices.

Use store brands whenever possible

Store brands are almost always the same as name-brand products with a different package and can save you 50% or more. Remember, store brands are made by the same name-brand manufacturers.

Choose laundry detergent for cold water

Use laundry detergent with enzymes that works in cold water. Enzymes make the product clean better, even in cold water. By choosing a store-brand version, you can save even more. Not only are you saving on your grocery bill but cutting your electricity bill at the same time by washing in cold water.

Buy bar soap instead of shower gel

Bar soap typically costs between $0.50 and $.75 a bar and will last approximately the same amount of time as a $6.00-8.00 bottle of shower gel. That's a savings of 90%!

Don't buy bottled water

There are many more economical choices that are also far more environmentally friendly. Did you know that most bottled water is simply filtered tap water? Faucet or pitcher filters do a great job of purifying your tap water, so it is equivalent in every way to bottled water.

There are a couple of good brands available at your local grocery or discount department store. Brita and Pur both make good quality water filtering products. Fill up a pitcher of filtered water and put it in your refrigerator and you'll have a ready supply of cold, filtered water at any time. If you need to take drinking water with you, fill up a reusable water bottle!

Take advantage of sales and specials

Take a quick look at the local grocery store ad before your shopping trip. You can plan meals based on what might be on special that week and save.

Buy meat in bulk packages

This option is almost always cheaper per pound. You can split up the package and freeze in meal-size portions. Choosing chicken or turkey over beef for most of your meals will also save since poultry prices are significantly lower per pound. During the winter, many stores sell whole turkeys and hams at significantly reduced prices. Time to stock up and freeze!

Use coupons whenever you can

You can find them in your weekly store ads as well as online. There are some great apps for couponing if you just can't bring yourself to clipping out those paper ones. There are a few good ones to check out.

Grocery iQ (Android) has many features to make your grocery shopping a breeze. You can build your list, check for applicable coupons, and even add your store's loyalty card if it has one. The great thing about this app is that it can be shared among family members.

Another good choice is Ibotta. With this app, you select coupons from the list of available coupons. When you finish your shopping trip, you will scan in the bar codes from the product and the receipt to redeem your coupon. Once your account reaches $20, you can get your cash back from PayPal.

Finally, SnipSnap (iOS) is an app that allows you to scan and upload coupons from multiple print sources to add to the already huge database of coupons available.

Financial Services

There are many banks and credit unions that offer no-fee checking and savings accounts. Just be sure to check and make sure you meet any requirements such as minimum deposit amounts, etc. Unless you have a good reason for using a bank, a credit union will almost always give you better rates on products such as CDs, loans, investment services, and often pay interest on checking accounts. I've even gotten great deals on insurance products through my credit union.

When making your choice of financial institution, be careful to look at their fee schedule. Are they going to charge you for using ATMs? Besides that, I have found that the customer service at a credit union is far better than I've experienced at any bank – because the credit unions are non-profits!

If you use online banking exclusively, there are many high-yield savings accounts available that pay over 20 times what the typical savings account pays. Go to bankrate.com to check out some of the most popular high-yield accounts ranked in order of interest rate. Currently, Vio Bank, Citibank, and HSBC Direct top the list with rates over 2%.

Medical

Medical cost increases have risen faster than household income over the last several decades. Currently, the annual cost per person tops $10,000. The number of people with chronic illnesses such as diabetes and heart disease has increased and so have the costs of treating these diseases. But many of these expensive to treat illnesses are preventable!

Live a healthy lifestyle
Simple lifestyle changes to reduce your chance of dealing with a chronic disease can keep your overall health care costs down. Eating a healthy diet, drinking plenty of water, and getting some exercise are the key. Getting annual checkups with your primary care physician, dentist, and ophthalmologist is important to help you prevent disease and treat problems while they are small. These costs are minimal compared to what you would pay should a health problem get out of hand.

Choose your medical plan wisely
You probably have a choice of medical plans. Do you take the time to understand your choices and the costs involved? It seems overwhelming to read through the pages and pages of lists and costs and try to determine what your best choice is. However, it is worth it. You need to know up front what your plan covers and what it does not – and what your deductibles and co-pays should be for things such as routine exams, tests, prescriptions, and hospitalization. Think about what your current medical needs are and select a plan that best fits with your needs. Of critical importance is understanding what is considered in-network and out of network. Many medical plans out there won't pay a cent towards an out of network expense. Within your medical plan, you may have the ability to shop around for services such as testing and imaging. Take advantage of these and cut costs!

Take advantage of FSA/HSA plans

Do you have an FSA or HSA account to save pre-tax money for medical expenses? If your employer offers medical plans, they likely also offer one or both types of accounts. Either of these types of accounts can be used to pay for copays, deductibles, many prescription drugs, and other medical costs. However, the two types of accounts differ in significant ways.

The FSA is a Flexible Savings Account. You can save money annually on a pre-tax basis to go towards medical expenses. Currently the maximum amount you can contribute in 2019 is $2700. The downside of an FSA account is if you don't use all the money in the account within the plan year, you lose it. However, a few plans do allow a rollover of up to $500 from one year to the next.

In order to contribute to a Health Savings Account (HSA) you must also have a high-deductible medical plan. The HSA accounts are like the FSA in that you can save money pre-tax to pay for medical expenses. HSA accounts are also available through many banks if your employer does not offer them. Contribution rates for these accounts are much higher than FSAs, the current maximum for 2019 is $3500 for an individual or $7000 for a family. Savers over the age of 50 can contribute up to $1000 more per year.

One great benefit of a Health Savings Account is that most offer an investment option. You can invest in mutual fund and bond options inside the account, providing you with an opportunity to grow your money tax-free. You will never pay taxes on either your principal investment or the gains when you withdraw the money.

Save on Prescription drugs

Choose generics over name brand prescription medicines and take advantage of 90-day mail-order offers that give you a discounted price. Generics cost but a fraction of the cost of name-brand medicines and contain the exact same active ingredients as the name-brand medicine. They may differ in subtle ways such as color, shape, and packaging.   When generic choices aren't available, use a GoodRx prescription drug savings card instead of your insurance and save up to 80%. There is no fee, prepayment or credit card required to sign up and GoodRx is accepted at over 70,000 pharmacies, including CVS, Walmart, Walgreens, Kroger, Safeway, and Albertsons. Visit GoodRx.com to sign up!

Clothing and Shoes

You may find great deals at the end of each season – keep your eye out for sales and use your store loyalty card if you have one for extra savings. There are certain days of the year when you can find great bargains at just about every retail store - think Labor Day, President's Day, Black Friday and the day after Christmas - when stores discount popular items to increase sales.

Consider shopping at discount stores for clothing and shoes. Large retailers like Walmart and Target carry clothing and shoes at discount prices. Smaller specialty stores like Famous Footwear have a business model that offers discounted prices lower than the suggested retail prices every day. You can increase your savings by taking advantage of advertised sales and using your loyalty points.

Ross Dress for Less is the largest off-price discount clothing store chain that has a similar business model. Ross can offer lower prices due to their no-frills approach to their stores. Skimping on fancy store furnishings means more savings for their customers.

Miscellaneous

Depending on your situation, some of the categories listed below as part of "Miscellaneous" may, in fact, consume a large enough portion of your budget to be included as a separate budget category. For example, we have 5 dogs and a bird, so Pets is a separate budget category for us. You be the judge.

Dry clean at home

Don't pay for expensive dry cleaning! You can do it yourself with a $10 Dryel or Woolite at-home dry cleaning kit. Just toss 4-5 garments in the specially designed bag with the unfolded dry-cleaning sheet and run on the high heat cycle for 30 minutes in your dryer. Remove items immediately and hang to avoid wrinkles. You could pay anywhere between $6-$10 per item at a dry-cleaning store. Doing your own dry cleaning at home can save you well over 90% of the cost!

Join your public library

Why pay for the latest bestseller when your public library will loan it to you for free? Join your public library to enjoy access to all kinds of media; books, e-books, audiobooks, music, and movies. It costs nothing to join and there's plenty to choose from!

Pets

Get a discount every day on pet food and supplies by ordering online at Chewy.com. They stock food, treats, toys, and more for dogs, cats, fish, reptiles, horses, birds, and other small pets such as rabbits, ferrets, guinea pigs, etc. You'll save 50% off your first Autoship order. After that, you can expect to see at least 5-10% savings on every Autoship order with no charge for shipping. You can always change the items in your Autoship basket and the date you want your order shipped.

Besides these ongoing deals, there are many items on sale that you can choose from at deep discounts. The site includes an online pharmacy as well, so you can order your pet medications at a discount too. I love Chewy.com because it not only saves me a lot of money, but it saves me time as well. Orders are delivered within a day or two of shipping right to my door and I don't have to make a trip to the pet store!

Skip the gym membership

You don't need a fancy, expensive gym membership. Invest in a good pair of athletic shoes and get moving! Walking, jogging, playing tennis or basketball, riding a bike, and more can all be accomplished without paying hundreds or thousands of dollars a year.

Like to workout at home? Go to YouTube to find just about any kind of workout you're looking for. From Yoga to kettlebells, Zumba to Jillian Michaels, body weight workouts to step routines - you will find something on YouTube to meet your needs!

Education

The costs of higher education have skyrocketed in the past few decades. However, there are ways to save big bucks on an education - especially if you plan. Have children you're saving for? Set up a 529 investment account to make contributions that will grow tax-deferred like a Traditional IRA, but the withdrawals are tax-free for any qualified educational expenses.

While they're in high school, students can earn college credit for taking and passing AP exams and CE courses. In recent years, many high schools have partnered with local community colleges to offer parallel courses so that high school students can graduate with an Associate's degree.

There is also the College Level Examination Program (CLEP) available whereby students can pay a fee (currently $89) to take any of dozens of tests to earn college credit. That's only a small fraction of what you would pay at a 4-year college to take an equivalent course. Over 2900 colleges and universities accept CLEP scores for credit. Get more information about this program at clep.collegeboard.org.

Finally, it is much less expensive to take equivalent courses at a community college. If you are interested in going further and getting a 4-year degree, be sure to coordinate with the appropriate academic advisor at that institution to be sure of which credits will transfer.

Do it yourself

Ever have things around the house that need fixing? Doing small repair jobs yourself will save you the expense of paying for someone else's time to do it. If you are handy, this can save you a lot of money in the long run.

We had a dishwasher freeze up one extremely cold winter. It would have cost hundreds of dollars to have a serviceman come out and repair it. We found the part for $32 and a YouTube video that showed us how to replace it. Saved 90%!

There are many repair and maintenance items around the house that you can do yourself if you take the time to learn how. Here are a few:
- Change your own vehicle oil and air filter
- Swimming pool maintenance
- Painting projects
- Mowing the lawn
- Trimming shrubs and small trees
- Repairing fences
- Repairing/replacing tile

Save your money for the big repair bills!

Here's how some of our monthly budget items were reduced when we cut costs in the past year using some of the ideas described above:

Monthly bill	Before	After
Auto loan (traded)	346	248
Groceries	800	500
Cell Phone	175	28
Gym	132	0
Cable TV	75	0
Pool service	100	0
Lawn service	115	0
Medical	602	470
Water/Trash	115	101
Total	**2609**	**1447**

This is of course not everything, but in just these categories of the budget you can see we have been able to pare down over $1150!

Chapter 5 – Habits for Boosting Income

Regardless of where you are in life – just starting out, mid-career, preparing for retirement, or already retired – there are lots of ways you can increase your income! Developing multiple streams of income is the smart way to keep you out of the poorhouse and living a comfortable lifestyle for the rest of your life.

On the job

Working overtime at your current job or taking on a side job can boost your income both now and, in the future, as your contributions to Social Security and perhaps a pension plan will increase along with your paycheck. Similarly, you can ask for a raise and apply for promotions when the opportunity comes up. Doing everything you can to increase your paycheck throughout your career will go a long way towards financial security for you in the short-term and provide a bigger social security benefit and pension (if applicable) when you retire.

Working longer can also boost your income long-term. Even working one additional year longer than what you maybe had planned can bring both short and long-term benefits. Put off taking social security as long as you can. Each year you delay beyond 62 gets you an approximately 8% increase in your social security check. You can't beat that interest rate anywhere else! Delaying social security to your full retirement age (67 for most) will get you a 30% bigger check than if you take it at age 62. Maximize your benefit by taking social security at 70. Go to ssa.gov to set up an account online and see a current estimate of benefits.

Take on a side gig
Other than taking on a part-time job (which you can do), there are other paying opportunities you can do on a more flexible basis. Get paid to take surveys, participate in consumer panels, even to watch particular TV shows or videos! Get yourself hooked up at InboxDollars.com to find some of these opportunities.

Passive income options

Passive income is income that continues after the bulk of the work is done. Your money does the work for you! There are entire books written about this subject, if you're interested.

Online
There are lots of interesting ways to make passive income online. Upload videos to YouTube, write a blog, develop an online course, or run a website and get paid repeatedly by advertisers running ads on your site without you doing any more work. Self-published e-books (like this one) are a great way to go if you're willing to do a little research.

Real estate

Probably the most obvious cash-generating investment is rental property. If you can afford to buy distressed properties at a bargain to fix up and rent – this could be a great passive income generator for you! There are real-estate management firms you can hire to take care of the maintenance and leasing of your property so you can be entirely hands-off.

If you like the idea of investing in real estate but don't have the up-front cash investment that it requires, consider Fundrise. You can invest as little as $500 in a real estate portfolio that has historically generated 8.7%-12.4% annual returns. Like full-service investment firms, Fundrise offers a choice of portfolios based on your investing style. Check it out and see if this is a good option for you at Fundrise.com.

Rent out space in your home with Airbnb

You can make hundreds a night for space you're already paying for. If you enjoy hosting guests this option might be right for you! List your space at Airbnb.com.

Rent your auto

In major metropolitan areas you can list your car or truck for rent on turo.com. Check it out to see what your vehicle can earn for you! Rent your RV. Your RV probably spends most of its time sitting in storage. Why not be earning at the same time? Go to rvshare.com to list yours for rent.

Investments

Investments, CDs and high-yield savings accounts are great ways to let your money earn for you. Dividend-earning stocks and ETFs will pay out monthly income. It's your choice whether to cash out or reinvest your earnings. Consider purchasing an annuity if you are looking for an investment that can provide a guaranteed lifetime passive income stream for you and your surviving spouse. These are policies sold through insurance companies and highly regulated by the insurance industry. Many offer desirable perks, such as death benefits and immediate payout options should you be diagnosed with a terminal illness

Use cashback rewards cards and apps

Free money here! If you use a credit card to pay bills, why not use one that pays you back? If you're shopping online, shop through a cashback site like TopCashback.com to earn rewards in cold, hard cash! It is free to join and can earn you cash back at over 3500 stores..

Start a business

Start your own business from a hobby you enjoy. If you're into photography, sell photos online. There are over a dozen sites online that will buy them. Give it a try with one of these great sites: 123rf.com, depositphotos.com, shutterstock.com.

Enjoy pets? Try pet sitting or dog walking. Sign up at petsitter.com or care.com for pet care jobs. Specialize in pet photography. Make homemade pet treats or other pet products to sell. The pet business is booming – use your love of pets to become a part of it!

Are you a creative type? Make jewelry, sculpture, or art? Sell your work on Etsy online or to local shops. Teaching others how to enjoy a hobby is another way you can make money and have fun, too! Create an online course or YouTube video series for extra cash. Maybe you're interested in one of the hundreds of franchise opportunities that are available. Search through ideas at franchisegator.com or franchisedirect.com for something that interests you. After you've had your fun, sell your business!

Sell your old stuff

Do you have old stuff lying around in closets or stored in the garage that you never use anymore? Most of us do. Consider having a garage sale or sell it online. Post it for sale on Craig's List. Relieve yourself of the clutter and get some cash in the process!

Chapter 6 – Habits to Reduce Debt

In the previous two chapters, you discovered many ways to both spend less of your money and increase your income. Having done this, you should now have more wiggle room in your budget to take that extra money - however much it is - and use it to pay down your debt. Here are a few things you can do that will help speed up the process.

Consolidation loans

If you have a job and decent credit, you can rid yourself of those high-interest credit card debts with a consolidation loan. Not only does this reduce the number of bills you pay every month, it reduces the total amount of money you'll shell out over time and gives you a definite date when it will be paid off. Apply at your bank or credit union first as they often reward their own customers with a lower rate on a personal loan. Bonus! Your credit rating is nearly guaranteed to increase by taking this step.

0% credit card transfers

If you're like me and have at least one inactive credit card, then you are getting offers in the mail to transfer your higher interest card balances at a low interest rate – maybe even a 0% rate. This can be worth it if there is little or no transfer fee and the offer gives you at least 12 months at the 0% rate. This can give you time to pay down the balance without the additional interest fees to pay. A caution – be sure to pay close attention to the terms as the interest rate after the time has expired may be higher than you are willing to pay.

Paydown methods

There are three main methods generally used to pay down debt. They require that you have some discretionary cash every month to use for debt – a good number to shoot for is $250-$500. If you don't have an extra $250, find a way to get it. The 3 methods differ in what order you pay down your debts.

The first way to pay down debts is to start with the debt with the highest interest rate. This requires you have a list of your debts, ranked in order of interest rate. As you pay off the first debt by paying an extra $250 every month, use the money that would have gone towards that payment plus your extra $250 to add to your next highest interest rate debt. And so on, until all your debts are paid. Mathematically this is the fastest way you can pay off debt.

Another way to tackle your debt is to start with the smallest debt, regardless of interest rate. This method also requires you have a list of debts - ranked in order by size of the total amount owed. Pay an extra $250-$500 towards the smallest debt until it is paid off, then add that payment to your next smallest debt until it is paid off. Many people are more successful with paying down debt this way because there is a feeling of satisfaction early on when the first debt is paid. The reward that comes with paying off the first debt motivates you even more to pay off the second.

One other method that some people try is paying extra on all their debts every month. This method tends to be less successful as you don't see much change in your bills month to month and it takes much longer to get a bill paid off.

Finally, what has worked best for me is to list my debts in order of size and work on paying off one of the smaller debts with the largest monthly payment first. This method provides more bang for the buck since losing one of your larger payments first will give you extra room in your budget to work on paying down other debts.

Chapter 7 – Habits for Saving and Investing

Now that you have slashed your spending (I hope you have!) using some of the ideas in Chapter 4, have boosted your income and paid off most of your debts, you now have room in your budget to save and invest for some of those long-term goals.

Establish an emergency fund

How much should you save for emergencies? Most estimates suggest that you have 3-6 months of salary saved in an emergency fund. Establish this savings fund first before you begin investing. You don't want to have to rely on credit cards in case of emergencies – and there are always going to be emergencies! Put this money away in a separate savings account and don't touch that money except for emergencies. Now you are ready to invest.

Invest for retirement

Retirement planning experts recommend you save 10-15% of your income towards retirement throughout the entirety of your working life in order to live comfortably in retirement. Depending on how close you are to retiring, you may want to increase that. If you want your money to grow over time (who doesn't?), consider investing in 401K, 403b, Traditional IRA, Roth IRA and Health Savings Accounts – whichever are available to you.

If you have young children and need to save for their college expenses, there are 529 College Savings plans that you can invest in with different portfolio options to grow your money. The IRS allows folks over 50 to increase contributions to HSA, 401K, 403b, and IRA accounts. Take advantage of this if you can and maximize your contributions during what is most likely your highest earning years.

During retirement, your biggest cost will most likely be healthcare. If you can't maximize contributions to all your investment accounts, prioritize maximizing your HSA. Contributions are made pre-tax and you will never pay income tax on the growth of your money (if you have investment options) or the principal when it is withdrawn for healthcare reasons. This makes an HSA perhaps your most important investment tool for retirement. If you are working and have a high-deductible health care plan, you are eligible to contribute to an HSA.

You can choose to work with a full-service investment firm and pay a bit more. Edward Jones, Morgan Stanley, and Merrill Lynch are some well-known full-service brokerages where you can work directly with a financial advisor to set up accounts and manage your investments. This is a great choice if you are new to investing or don't have the time to take on investment research for yourself. It never hurts to have an expert on your side!

If you are more independent-minded and like doing your own research, consider a do-it-yourself investment account with a discount broker online. There are several good choices of low-cost investment brokerages where you can set up a Traditional or Roth IRA and select your own investments. Vanguard, TD Ameritrade, Schwab, Fidelity, T. Rowe Price are a few better-known examples of discount brokers.

Warren Buffett, probably the most well-known investor of our times, suggests investing in a low-cost index fund at a discount brokerage and maintaining your investment long-term to maximize your money's growth. Next to low-cost index funds, there's another great choice if you want to set-it and forget it. Invest in a target date retirement fund. Fees are a bit more expensive, but the target date fund is aggressively managed to more effectively manage risk and make more conservative investment choices (more bonds, fewer stocks) the closer you get to your retirement date.

Automate savings and investments

Make contributions to savings and investment plans automatic by setting up withdrawals directly from your paycheck or checking account on payday. If you are making monthly contributions to a 401K, 403b, or IRA with mutual funds, stocks, or ETFs - more shares are purchased at lower prices rather than higher prices than if you made less frequent contributions. This is called Dollar Cost Averaging and helps mitigate the negative effects of large swings in the market. By making contributions every payday, you won't see the money and are less likely to miss it.

Don't give away free money

If your employer offers a match program for a retirement fund (401K, 403b), make sure you make the appropriate contributions to receive the entire amount of the match. Otherwise, you are throwing away free money! Many do not take advantage of the employer match program because it can be confusing. By contributing too little, too early, or too late, you may miss out.

Be sure to ask your employer how the match is calculated and when the match is applied. Oftentimes an employer will offer a match rate of 50% on a percentage of your salary. Figure out what that maximum match will be for you.

For example, if your employer will match 50% on a 3% contribution on a $50,000 annual salary you would first calculate your minimum contribution:

3% of $50,000=$1500

In this case, your minimum contribution to receive a match is $1500.

Divide this number by 12 to find out your monthly contribution rate:

$1500/12=$125

Then apply the 50% employer match:

50% of $1500=$750

$750 is the maximum amount per month your employer will contribute on your behalf.

This scenario shows that to receive the maximum match, you must make a minimum contribution of $125 every month. Unfortunately, some think it is possible to still receive the maximum match from an employer if they contribute less some months of the year and make up for it the rest of the year. It doesn't work that way – match amounts are generally determined by the monthly payroll and the cap applied every month. Besides getting free money that will help your investments grow faster, another benefit of an employer match program is that the money your employer contributes will not count against your annual maximum contribution rate.

Wrap-up

I hope after reading this book you have learned many new money habits to help you budget, set goals, and cut costs so you have the freedom to reduce your debt and save for the things you really want. As I stated at the beginning of this book, your money is *your* money so the choices are yours. If you enjoyed this book and were able to take away some ideas that helped you with your personal finances, I'd appreciate it if you visited the book's page on Amazon and left a review.

Resources

www.microsoft.com
www.mint.com
www.youneedabudget.com
www.mvelopes.com
www.quicken.com
www.moneydance.com
www.countabout.com
www.personalcapital.com
https://www.annualcreditreport.com/index.action
www.bankrate.com
www.nerdwallet.com/insurance
www.anylist.com
www.chewy.com
https://clep.collegeboard.org
www.ssa.gov
www.fundrise.com
www.airbnb.com
www.turo.com
www.rvshare.com
www.inboxdollars.com
www.topcashback.com
www.123rf.com
www.depositphotos.com
www.shutterstock.com
www.petsitter.com
www.care.com
www.franchisegator.com
www.franchisedirect.com

Made in the USA
Monee, IL
13 January 2020